THE J DISTILLER'S GUIDE

RAISE THE BAR

AND DIY BARTENDER: COCKTAILS FOR THE HOMEMADE

HOME DISTILLING
STUDYING & WORKBOOK

BY

JIM O'BRIEN

SECOND EDITION

ISBN: 9781719894876

LEGAL & DISCLAIMER

TABLE OF CONTENTS

A NOTE TO READERS

Dear readers,

For most of you, this is my first book. I hope in this book you can find the answers to your questions and receive some advice. All of this based on the author's personal experience and every sentence in this book is important. It's a book that contains a very few terms. It can be easily understood by anybody.

Thank you, dear readers,
I highly appreciate your estimation of my work!

Sincerely yours, Jim O'Brien

Why Home Distillation?

Home distillation isn't for everyone. While some homebrewers are happy enough with beer or

wine, others want to take it a step further, by distilling those grain and fruit mashes and concentrating their alcohol into true spirits worthy of any bar.

Should I Try Home Distillation?

Ultimately, only you can decide if the time, effort, and money are worth it for you to try your hand at this. It does require a great deal of research and learning beforehand, and isn't the cheapest hobby to get started on - but for those who stick with it, home distillation can quickly grow into a true passion. For some hobbyists, it's become a livelihood or viable side-job.

Need some convincing? As any home distiller will tell you, this process is:

• Economical. Aside from the initial cost of materials and ingredients, distilling your own alcohol costs far less than buying it, especially if you plan to distill alcohol with cheap sources (potatoes, grains, etc.). Jars and bottles can be reused if desired, and purchased in bulk; ingredients can also be ordered wholesale, especially botanicals and spices.

- Customizable. Ever wonder what fresh peach moonshine would taste like? What about apple-blackberry rum with a ginger and lavender infusion? When it comes to home distillation, the sky's the limit: let your imagination run wild. You can combine virtually any ingredients and flavors to create truly one-of-a-kind distillations you'd never find on store shelves.

- Fun! Most importantly, distillation is enjoyable. While some folks might try it and decide it's not for them, most people who take the time to research thoroughly, buy materials, build the still, and prepare proper washes, mashes, or worts, have a genuine interest and budding passion in this activity. For them, this can be an incredibly fun and intriguing process, even when they're still learning the ropes.

Making Liquor at Home...Legally?

This is the biggest question when it comes to home distillation: is it legal?

The short answer is, no. You can't simply buy or build a still and start distilling liquor in your garage without breaking the law.

The long answer! Maybe! It depends on your local laws, not just federal and state ones. We'll focus on mostly federal ones in this book, but distillers-in-training should research their county, and city laws, as well, to avoid any unexpected trouble. Your state laws matter, too, so take time to learn all the necessary regulations and requirements.

Note: Technically speaking, federal law prohibits distilling and drinking your own alcohol, no ifs, ands, or buts. There are ways around it, however, including obtaining the proper permits and, if need be, paying taxes.

Owning a still is not illegal, since people use it for other purposes, from decoration to distilling water. Many people falsely believe that stills under 1 gallon are legal, while anything larger isn't; stills of any size are legal to own. All stills over 1 gallon (and any used to make alcohol), however, are tracked by the Tobacco Tax and Trade Bureau, and all sellers of stills must report their customers' information to this agency if requested. Don't go on hearsay or internet grapevines: do your research for yourself, and consult local and state governments for clarification, if needed.

So, how can you make sure you're distilling within the law? Obtain a federal permit (either a federal fuel alcohol permit or a distilled spirits permit, as applicable); register your still with the TTB if it isn't already (if you purchased it from a manufacturer vs. building one yourself, it will already be registered); get a state permit, and any local ones you might need for your city and/or county. Additionally, certain spirits might require specific permits, depending on your area [1].

Below we've featured a list of all U.S. states and territories that, with the proper permits, DO allow home distillation.

Disclaimer: This is not a legal advice. Use your discretion when distilling and obtain all permits, forms, etc., to do so within federal and local laws.

1. "Is Making Moonshine Legal?" Clawhammer Supply, published January 11, 2013. Accessed June 13, 2017. https://www.clawhammersupply.com/blogs/moonshine-still-blog/7155304-is-making-moonshine-legal

The U.S. States and Territories that Allow Home Distillation

Alabama
Alaska
Arizona
Arkansas
California
Colorado
Connecticut
Delaware
District of Columbia
Florida
Georgia
Guam
Hawaii
Idaho
Indiana
Iowa
Kansas
Kentucky
Louisiana
Maine
Maryland
Massachusetts
Michigan
Minnesota
Mississippi
Montana
Nebraska
Nevada
New Hampshire
New Jersey
New Mexico

New York
North Carolina
North Dakota
Northern Marianas Islands
Ohio
Oklahoma
Oregon
Pennsylvania
Rhode Island
South Carolina
South Dakota
Tennessee
Texas
Utah
Vermont
Virginia
Virgin Islands
Washington
West Virginia
Wisconsin
Wyoming

For Canada, Ontario is the only area to allow home distillation.

Note: laws in these areas allow home distillation for PERSONAL use. Selling alcohol you've made yourself is an entirely different process, requires far more than the typical local, state, and federal permits, and will be covered more in Chapter 13.

CHAPTER 1. THE BASIC PRINCIPLES OF DISTILLATION

Distillation is the physical separation (i.e. not chemical) of a mixture. In the case of alcoholic distillation, you're separating alcohol from water, by taking advantage of the two components' different boiling points.

Because water boils at 212 degrees Fahrenheit, it doesn't become a vapor/gas until after ethanol does, which boils at 173 degrees. This means alcohol vapors leave the liquid mixture first. A still is designed to capture these vapors and cool them back into a liquid form, while leaving as much of the water (and other ingredients) behind as possible. The result is a purer, stronger alcohol than what you started with[1].

Types of Distillation

Whether you're distilling water, alcohol, or any kind of mixture, the principles of this process are essentially the same.

---

[1] "Distillation: Main Principles." Rhum Agricole. Accessed June 13, 2017. http://www.rhum-agricole.net/site/en/fab_distillation

Simple distillation is the process of extracting a liquid by taking advantage of its boiling point being lower than the rest of the mixture, which means the desired element will evaporate first, so you can collect it.

There's also steam distillation, which is sometimes used to purify water; this tends to involve some contamination because some impurities will have a lower or similar boiling point to water and end up in the final distillation.

Fractional distillation, which is often used to purify oil and other fuels, involves a much longer reflux column that gets cooler near the top. As the mixture heats and elements evaporate, some will rise higher in the column in others, which means they'll re-condense at a different point in the tower. With multiple condenser tubes attached, one can distill several elements at once without having to monitor the temperature rigidly and switch collection containers. This method divides the mixture into its elements (or "fractions") rather than pulling one element and leaving the rest to condense back into the mixture.

Advanced distillers sometimes use fractional stills for their alcohol, so that the foreshots, hearts, and tails are separated into their own containers. In a reflux column, you have to collect these elements separately.

All three methods have the same basic idea: by vaporizing some elements of a mixture, you can isolate those elements while leaving behind the parts you don't want in your final distillation.

Since this book focuses on a basic reflux still, we'll take a more in-depth look at the principles of simple distillation.

Simple Distillation in Detail

How easily something turns into vapor is called its volatility, which means it has a lower threshold for its vapor pressure to exceed atmospheric pressure. In short, the more volatile a substance, the lower its boiling point. In alcohol distillation, you have three main volatile substances: ethanol, methanol, and water.

Methanol is easily evaporated; its boiling point is 148.5 degrees Fahrenheit. Ethanol - the primary ingredient in the final distillation - is next, with a boiling point of 173.1 degrees. Finally, there's water, which doesn't evaporate until it reaches 212 degrees.

To distill the ethanol and get as little water as possible, you'll want to heat your mixture above 173 degrees, but below 212. This also means you'll get toxic methanol in your distillation - but, if you increase your heat relatively slowly, you'll be able to extract the methanol before the ethanol begins to come out. Chart your still's temperature; when it reaches 148.5, but before it reaches 173.1, methanol will begin to evaporate and recondense, dripping into your collection container. This is known as the foreshots and heads of a distillation, and it's good practice to throw this portion away. For every 5 gallons of wash you're distilling, discard the first 50 mL distilled.

In time, you'll learn what the foreshots smell and look like, and be able to distinguish them without guesswork or a hydrometer.

Once the methanol has been distilled and discarded, ethanol will begin to evaporate and condense. This is the portion you want to collect. Some water will be mixed in your final distillation, which is normal (and preferable, to obtain a proper drinking proof).

So why can't you just keep your still at exactly 173.1 degrees, so you get pure ethanol but no water? The answer to this, in the simplest of terms, is that you can control your still's temperature—but not your wash mixture inside it. Even if you don't change your heat source at all, the wash will continue to grow hotter, in part because its total volume is decreasing over time (so the heat disperses throughout the mixture more quickly and completely; it's a bit like waiting for one cup of water to boil instead of an entire pot's worth).

That said, it is possible-and advisable-to try and steady your temperature throughout a distillation. If you can maintain a temperate between 173.1 and about 185 degrees Fahrenheit, you'll end up with a much stronger, less watered-down distillation when the process is complete. Once the mixture starts to heat up regardless of adjustment, you'll already be separating out the tails (a usually unusable, undrinkable portion most distillers discard).

It can take a great deal of practice to adjust and maintain proper temperatures while distilling, but a complete understanding of the distillation process is an excellent place to start! When you know exactly what's going on inside your still, you can better predict and comprehend what needs to be changed for the highest quality result possible.

CHAPTER 2. OVERVIEW OF THE DISTILLING PROCESS AND TECHNIQUES

You're probably eager to build a still and get right to work, but hold off a little longer! Even knowing what distillation is, it helps to understand how these principles apply to distilling alcohol. Knowing this process inside and out will help you troubleshoot any problems that might come up and, ultimately, make you a better distiller as time goes on.

What Happens Inside a Still?

The body of a still (also called a vat) contains the wash, the liquid portion of a fermented mixture. The vat is heated, which increases the ingredients' pressure. As soon as it exceeds the atmospheric pressure, these elements begin to evaporate.

The evaporations rise to the top of the vat, where they become trapped in the reflux column. The earliest vapors will make it through this column and into a condenser tube, which is lined with a water jacket-imagine a tube, surrounded by water within another tube. The water cools this vapor so it condenses back into its liquid state. It then drips down a collection tube into a container. In the case of alcohol distillation, this product is ethanol. It evaporates first and makes it through the column with ease.

So what about the vapors that follow? Thanks to the packing material inside, which provides a high surface area; these vapors can condense into a liquid state again and fall back down into the wash. This reflux is mostly water, which, because of its higher boiling point, takes longer to evaporate and thus has a higher vapor pressure, which means it would require higher levels of heat to reach the condenser. When distilling, one must take care not to heat the wash too high; this will cause the water to evaporate at the same rate as the alcohol, which will mix too much water in the final distilled product. A common sign of too-high heat is when a distillation's ABV (its alcohol percentage by volume) is much lower than you expected. This can also happen when you distill the wash longer than you should or "run it dry." Additionally, the sediment of your fermented product can burn and crust the vat, which can harm your still and taint your distillation or alter its flavor.

In short, stills do not produce alcohol: they make it more concentrated by volume. By using heat to take advantage of the elements' different boiling points, you can separate the elements you want – alcohol - from those you don't, like water and the sediment of your original ingredients, like corn or barley. Be aware that even distilled alcohol has some water in it; this is inevitable and actually preferable. Pure alcohol is dangerous to drink, but that little bit of water that sneaks through will lower the alcohol percentage just enough to make it safe for consumption.

Prior to distillation, there's the equally important process of fermentation; before that, creating a quality wash; and, before even that, shopping for quality ingredients. Alcohol distillation is truly a craft of care and is not for the impatient.

Distilling: an Overview of the Process

When you've got your fermented mash ready to go, your equipment sterilized and set up, you'll start distilling the liquid portion of your mash (known as the wash, once fermentation is complete) into its purer form, by extracting the alcohol from the mixture.

First, use a siphon to get your wash into the

still vat. You can do this with a siphon hose and start the suction yourself (with your mouth, draw the excess air out of the tube while one end is in the wash bucket/fermenter) or with a pump, which is much easier. This will create a vacuum within the tube and draw the liquid inside. Place the other end of the tube in the vat and allow the liquid to transfer from one container to the other. Take care that the end of the siphon tube is not in the bottom of the fermenter, where it can suck up excess sediment and yeast. Your goal is to get the liquid into the vat while leaving as much of this material behind as you can. When your vat is full, close up your still.

Next, you'll start your water. This will run cold water continuously to the condenser jacket so that your ethanol vapors in the condenser tube will cool down and drip into your collection jars. Make sure the return hose leads to a clear drain, such as in a utility sink. The water will run the entire distillation process.

Once your water is running and draining properly, you'll start your heat source. This part should not be rushed - while it's tempting to crank up that heat and get things going at full-steam (literally), you need to carefully monitor your temperature. This will vary a little depending on your wash, but should not exceed 212 degrees Fahrenheit. In fact, anything over 173 but below 200 will probably work just fine. Your goal is to get your distillation's output at 1 drop every 1-3 seconds. Anything faster than that indicates a too-high temperature and means your distillation is probably getting a lot more water mixed in than it should.

Your first collection will be the foreshots and heads. This is roughly the first 50mL distilled from a 5-gallon wash and will smell very harsh (in time, you'll be able to distinguish by scent; in the meantime, you can use a hydrometer, if you'd like). The foreshots contain very high levels of methanol, which can be toxic. Discard this portion of your distillation and place a clean collection jar under the tube.

Do not leave your still unattended, even for a moment. This is high-proof alcohol, which can and will act as an accelerant if it comes in contact with heat or flame. You should also be watching for any leaks or signs of excessive pressure in your still, even if you've distilled hundreds of times before with no problem.

As each collection container fills, move your jars (unsealed) to a work surface far away from the still. A place outside of the stillhouse is best, if possible. Do not seal your jars yet; they still have heat and vapors coming off them, and these need to escape. Wait at least an hour before putting the lids on your collection jars.

Throughout the distillation process, take regular readings to check the alcohol content. If it's very low, adjust your heat accordingly.

Do not run your still dry - heating the last bit of a wash, which usually contains some sediment, can damage your vat and change the composition of your distillation. The end of a distillation is a murky, sour liquid known as the tails, and should also be discarded; alternatively, you can cut your heat source off and stop distilling prior to the tails' formation. This can take some practice and requires calculating your wash's size and distillation time, so don't feel bad if you get a few tails mixed into your distillations by accident.

On that note, consider smaller containers for your initial distillations; if you accidentally get any tails in the final collection, you won't have to discard your previous ones.

After distillation is complete, allow your containers to gas off and then seal or transfer to intended bottles. Let your still cool before opening up the head and cleaning out the vat. You may have to clean your column, as well, and adjust/add packing materials. Sterilize your still before the next use, even if you plan on distilling a wash identical to the one before it; bacteria can still cross-contaminate batches, even if they were made at the same time with the same ingredients.

For more information on bottling, storage, and preservation of your distillations, consult Chapter 14.

CHAPTER 3. DISTILLING EQUIP-
MENT AND RAW MATERIALS

Before embarking on any new endeavor, you need hours of research and dedication—but you'll also need plenty of materials! Even if you plan on buying your still instead of building one yourself, the list of what you need to get started is quite extensive. If cost is a factor, consider bartering services or products you already own with other distillers.

You can also find used equipment from people who've tried distilling and decided it wasn't for them, or folks who've upgraded to more complicated setups and no longer need their old equipment. Just make sure to test all your equipment for leaks or damage, and sterilize thoroughly before use (although you sterilize all equipment, even brand-new items, before each and every use).

What You'll Need for Mashes and Washes

There's no way around it: Good distillations

start with good mashes and washes, and these start with good ingredients. Here's a list of the ingredients you might need to stock up on before you begin:

- Potatoes
- Raw sugar
- White granulated sugar
- Barley (usually malted)
- Maize
- Fruit (grapes, apples, etc.)
- Spices such as cinnamon, nutmeg, etc.
- Juniper berries (for gin)
- Plentiful water source
- Agave syrup (for agave shine/mock tequila)

You'll also need several fermenters, as only mash can ferment in each at a time, a process that takes weeks. This way, you'll be able to have several batches fermenting at once, so you can have washes to distill in succession instead of waiting several weeks in-between them.

Fermenters come in many shapes, sizes, and materials. Some even feature spigots for easy siphoning when it's time to transfer the wash to the still. Plastic is cheapest, but doesn't hold up as well over time; some distillers refuse to use plastic for anything being fermented longer than a week since it's more prone to evaporation.

You can get fermenters as tanks, kegs, small jugs, large jugs - there's a fermenter out there for every need and every budget. Choose one with a 5 gallon capacity for the recipes in this book; this is also the amount that will fit in your still, as per our instructions. If your still is larger or smaller, order a fermenter suited to that size.

Carboys are jugs with rubber stoppers and airlocks, so you can prevent bacteria from entering your fermentation. They also reduce the amount of oxygen trapped in the container, so your batch won't spoil due to oxidation. There are also stainless steel fermentation vats, which are pricey, but prevent evaporation and oxidation very effectively.

The cheapest option, overall, is a plastic fermenter bucket. For short-term fermentation (3 weeks or so), these are effective and work quite well. They're a favorite of beginners and experienced distillers alike because they're cost-effective and lightweight, as well as easy to clean. Their lids have airlocks to prevent excessive oxygen from seeping in, as well as germs.

For Your Still

If you're building your own still, you'll need a host of materials from copper pipes to soldering irons, to drill bits and rubber grommets. We'll cover this more in-depth in the next chapter.

Additionally, you should consider your "still-house." Will you use a garage? A well-ventilated basement? That old shed in the back of the yard? No matter where you choose, make sure it's an area with doors and windows to open, fans to increase airflow (so you don't inhale the fumes coming off the distillations), a heat source or ability to install one, and a water source, such as a hose. A utility sink can also be useful but isn't required.

Set up your workspace with tables to work on, an area for distillation collection jars (as well as an area far away from the still, for finished distillations to go until they're ready for sealing or bottling). You might need shelves for your tools and additional materials, as well as a dedicated spot for your hydrometer. To siphon your washes into the still, procure a good racking/siphon hose. These are typically sold in rolls, some as long as 100 feet.

You can keep a logbook nearby to record distillation dates and proofs; a whiteboard can be a good place for fermentation timelines and notes. Sticky notes on your fermenters, or chalkboard labels/reusable stickers, will help differentiate one wash from another.

If storing your fermenters in the stillhouse, try to keep them a good distance from the still until it's time to siphon.

CHAPTER 4. YOUR STILL: PRE-MADE, HALFWAY, OR FROM SCRATCH?

Stills can be (and have been) fashioned out of many materials, and modified in a multitude of ways to suit a distiller's needs and preferences. In this book, we'll focus on a column reflux still.

You'll need three basic parts for your column still: a vat, the column, and a condenser. You can buy stills fully assembled (online is easiest), purchase these pieces and assemble the still in a few simple steps, or - if you're so inclined - build the still yourself from start to finish.

There are some advantages to all these approaches. While a fully assembled still will save you a great deal of time, it does cost quite a bit - and, for hands-on learners, can rob distillers of the opportunity to learn how a still operates in and out.

Purchasing the components and putting them together yourself gives you some of both worlds: you get to peek inside your still and see what makes it tick while saving yourself some money and time. This can be beneficial for anyone who wants to be immersed in the process, but isn't exactly handy with soldering irons and drills.

Finally, there's the craftsman's delight: building your entire still from scratch. It's relatively easy with the proper design and instructions, and can be not only cost effective, but incredibly fun, as well. By building your still yourself, you'll gain an understanding of its function you might not gain from research alone.

Building Your Own Still[1]

- Materials:

  - One 1" to ½" reducing coupling
  - One 1" copper tube, 23" long (for condenser core)
  - Two ½" copper tube, 7" long (for column cooling tubes)
  - Four 1½" copper tube, 2½" long
  - One 1½" elbow
  - One 1½" to 1" reducing coupler
  - One 1½" copper pipe, 17½" long (for condenser jacket)
  - Two 1½ x 1½ x ½ tee fittings
  - Two 1½ end caps
  - One 2" copper tube, 36" long
  - One 2" copper tube, 3" long (nipple)
  - One 2" end cap
  - One 2" x 2" x 1½" tee fitting
  - Quality boiler made of stainless steel, such as a large commercial cooking pot, pressure cooker, or old beer keg

- Tools:

---

1   "How to Make a Reflux Still: Complete Plans," LearntoMoonshine.com. Published on November 29, 2014. Accessed June 14, 2017. http://learntomoonshine.com/how-to-make-a-reflux-still-complete-plans-to-build-a-homemade-still

- Hacksaw or pipe cutter
- Bench vise
- Drill press or electric drill
- Dremel tool or round file
- Metal drill bit set (or 5/8" and 1 1/8" metal hole saw)
- Compass
- Propane torch
- Tape measure
- Lead-free solder and flux
- Sand cloth or steel wool (or copper joint cleaning brush)

- Building the Top

  - Condenser
    - Cut a 23" section of 1" copper pipe.
    - Solder a 1½" x 1" reducing coupling to the 23" length of 1" copper pipe.
    - Solder the smaller (1" x ½") reducing coupling to the other end of the pipe.
    - Assemble condenser jacket:
    - Drill a 1 1/8" hole in one of the two end caps.
    - Drill a 5/8" hole in the other end cap.
    - Cut a 17½" length of the 1½" copper pipe.
    - Cut two sections (2½" each) of the 1½" copper pipe.
    - Assemble condenser jacket by placing condenser core inside the jacket to en-

sure it fits. Alter as needed until it does.
- Solder joints with a lead-free soldering iron.
- Put ½" copper tube (7" long) in the tee fittings on your condenser; solder into position.

○ Reflux Column
- Build column head.
  • Drill a 3/8" hole in the top of the 2" end cap, then put grommet and thermometer into the hole.
  • Position 3" long piece of 2" copper pipe into the top of 2x2x1½" tee and solder in place.
  • Fit cap on top of 3" copper pipe, but do not solder into position. This needs to be unsoldered so you can open it after use for cleanings and adjustments.
- Assemble column body.
  • Cut a 3' (foot) piece of the 2" copper pipe.
  • Measure from the bottom of pipe halfway (1.5') and place a mark. This will indicate the center point.
  • Measure from the center point up 9¼" and mark.
  • Measure from the center point down 9¼" and mark.

- Your two marks should align with the two cooling tubes attached to the condenser (both the higher and lower ones).
- With the two marks as your guide, drill two 5/8" diameter holes. These holes will go through both sides of the pipe.
- Push condenser through holes, then position the column head onto the top of the still's body.
- Attach the 1½" elbow and 1½" copper tubes from the tee joint on the top of the column to the top of the condenser.
- Solder all joints to secure.

○ Attach to the boiler

 - Note: Alter instructions as needed, depending on the type of boiler you picked. Some containers, like kegs, will also require mounting flanges.
 - To attach reflux column to the boiler:
   - Drill a 2 1/8" hole in the lid.
   - Push 3" of the copper column through the hole and Mig weld.
   - Attach the screen to the protruding 3" of copper pipe, then secure with a 2" stainless steel hose clamp. This will hold your column packing (next step)

in place.

- Choose a Column Packing
  - This is used to increase the surface area inside the column, so vapors have more places to condense. It increases the amount of "reflux" (i.e. gives water more opportunity to condense and fall back into the pot, instead of going into the condenser coil with ethanol vapors), which will give you a higher proof and better quality product.

  - You can use stainless steel scrubbing pads, marbles, broken safety glass from automobiles, glass beads, etc. Choose materials with high surface areas that are easy to remove for cleaning and replacement, but that won't release impurities or toxins into your distillation. Also, try to avoid materials that can be broken, melted, or rusted due to the high heat and moisture inside the still.

  - To pack the column:
    - Remove the cap. Make sure the screen on the bottom of the tower is firmly attached; this will hold the packing inside the tube and keep it from slipping out into the pot.
    - Add packing material to column until it's filled to just above the highest cooling tube.
    - Place cap back on top of the column.

- Choose a heat source.
  - Stove top
  - Propane boiler
  - Electric immersion heaters

- Hook still up to a water source
  - A garden hose is commonly used; some distillers also use hoses attached to utility sinks.
  - Attach a water source via the inlet of the condenser (i.e., the lower ½" copper tube located on the condenser). Hook another hose running to a drain on the upper copper tube of the condenser.

That's It! Now, How Do You Use it?

Once you've assembled your still (or purchased and unwrapped it; no shame) you're ready to distill!

Well,...almost ready. First, you'll need to test your still with water, to check for leaks and any construction issues, proper packing material choice, etc. You'll also need to sterilize the entire thing, to avoid contamination.

The first real step to quality distillation, though, is a quality wash. If you haven't yet learned how to make your own washes, mashes, worts, etc. (the fermented mixtures that will be distilled into concentrated spirits), that's your next assignment. We'll provide some basic wash recipes in the chapters to follow.

I Already Got the Wash, Now What?

After fermentation is complete and all your still pieces and containers are sterile, you can siphon the wash into your still and get started distilling.

- Prepare jars (even if you plan on bottling your alcohol, wide-mouthed glass containers are best for collection). Make sure you can access and switch the jars quickly and easily, and that your work area is clean and uncluttered. Follow all proper safety concerns (outlined in the next chapter) prior to distillation.

- Fill the pot with the wash. Use a siphon for this; do not pour.

- Run water source, so water jacket can effectively cool the condenser tube and condense the vapors that will be collecting in it.

- Heat wash to 180-200 degrees Fahrenheit (some require different temperatures). Too high will start to mix your vapors and produce a watered-down distillation. Note: you will always have some water in your distillation. This is normal and needed, so your alcohol can be safely consumed at a drinking proof. If you find your distillations have too low proofs (in other words, too much water), it's possible your temps are too high, or your column is not packed with enough materials to allow water vapor to re-condense and fall back into the wash.

- Water jacket will begin cooling ethanol vapors; you should see drops, dripping from condenser tube very soon after optimal temp is reached.

- Discard the first few mL of collection (50 mL per 20 L of wash); this is called the foreshots or heads, and it can contain a very high, potentially toxic, amount of methanol. Many stills are constructed to eliminate this, but it's a good safety practice regardless.

- In a new, clean jar, collect the middle portion of your distillation, known as the hearts. This is the true distillation and will look and smell pleasant.

- Most washes will also require discarding the final mL, known as the tails, which are often milky and will not smell like hearts, but rather sour. Some distillers describe this smell as wet dog or cardboard, or a very sour fruit smell.

- Until you can distinguish your foreshots and heads, hearts, and tails by smell and appearance, use a hydrometer to measure the alcohol content of the liquid. Foreshots will have very high ABV (alcohol by volume) percentages; hearts will have an optimal, "drinking proof" level, and tails will have a low reading.

CHAPTER 5. MAKE ROOM FOR MOONSHINE

We all know moonshine when we see it - clear or colored, flavored or plain, labeled or low-key...but almost always in a trademark mason jar. But what, exactly, is moonshine?

While the term can be slang for any high-proof, illegally made, or home-distilled alcohol, it's technically whiskey. This is because it's made with a corn mash. Unlike whiskey, however, it's not aged in barrels, which is how whiskey gets its color (before aging, whiskey is clear, just like moonshine).

Is the Stuff at the Store Really Moonshine?

The moonshine you see in the liquor store is not true moonshine, but rather, a legal version brought back for a growing trend. This new version is made

42

with a great deal of sugar and additives and has a considerably lower proof than the real deal (although some can be high, depending on state laws and regulations).

You might also notice "moonshine recipes" online, especially Pinterest. These are tasty concoctions and pretty clever substitutions - but not true moonshine. Instead, recipes like that are infusions with Ever-clear and other high-proof grain alcohols. A popular technique is to dissolve the candy in jars of this stuff or mix them with fruit syrups.

While there's nothing wrong with these variations, be aware that they aren't real moonshine, because they aren't high-proof corn-mash distillations.

Moonshine's Start

During the American Prohibition from 1920 to 1933, the sale and consumption of all alcohol were made illegal. Americans in the Appalachian states took to producing their own spirits, collectively known as moonshine (regardless of the alcohol's type). The people who crafted it were called moonrakers, because they had to work at night or in secrecy to avoid the law.

Another fun fact: Nascar, the popular racing sport of the American south, got its start during Prohibition, thanks to moonshine. The drivers who transported the illegal alcohol to other parts of the country were known as bootleggers, and were frequently caught by police; as a result, crime rings tried to hire only the fastest drivers and would hold races to find them. This, eventually, led to Nascar[1].

In some areas today, moonshine is legal - but with a hefty tax attached. This is largely due to the 2008 recession, which also pushed states to legalize and subsequently tax) marijuana, to revitalize the economy[2]. This might be why the trend has grown so much since then, and why corporations released so many "pseudo-shines" into markets where the real product wasn't legalized.

How Moonshine Is Made

Moonshine starts with a corn mash, sometimes containing other ingredients. It can have flavors infused during distillation, but most shiners add their infusions and extras afterward, for a truer profile—

---

1   Billock, Jennifer. "How Moonshine Bootlegging Gave Rise to Nascar." Published by the Smithsonian Magazine Online, Februrary 10, 2017. Accessed June 15, 2017. http://www.smithsonianmag.com/travel/how-moonshine-bootlegging-gave-rise-nascar-180962014/

2   "A Brief History of Moonshine." Published by Bullpen Rib House Online, September 14, 2014. Accessed June 15, 2017. http://www.killerribs.com/blog/2014/9/14/a-brief-history-of-moonshine

and many prefer to leave it as-is, in all its natural glory.

○ **Basic Corn Mash Recipe** [3]

- Ingredients:
  - 5 gallons of water (if using tap water, allow to sit in the open container for a few hours to remove chlorine)
  - 8 ½ lbs. of flaked maize/corn
  - 1 ½ lbs. of crushed malted barley
  - 1 packet of yeast (bakers is the most commonly used)

- Directions:
  - In a large stainless steel cooking pot on stove-top, heat water to 165 degrees Fahrenheit.
  - Kill heat; add corn and stir continuously for about five minutes, then only occasionally, until the temperature drops to 152 degrees Fahrenheit.
  - Stir in malted barley.
  - Cover and let sit for 90 minutes; stir every 15 minutes.
  - Let sit a few hours, until mixture reaches 70 degrees.
  - Add yeast. Aerate your mixture between two

3   "How to Make Moonshine, Part 1: the Mash." Published by Clawhammer Supply, March 29, 2013. Accessed June 16, 2017. https://www.clawhammersupply.com/blogs/moonshine-still-blog/3386482-how-to-make-moonshine-part-1-the-mash

containers (like 5-gallon plastic buckets); pour into one, then pour into the other, and repeat a few times.
- Pour mixture into the fermenter. Cap and add the airlock.
- Let sit for 2-3 weeks before distilling.

- To distill:
  - Siphon into the still. Make sure the remnants of your wash (ingredients, yeast, etc.) are left in the fermenter as much as possible.

○ **Sugar "Mash" Recipe4**

- Note: This is not true moonshine, but the product many people are familiar with nowadays. This is best if your intention for your moonshine is to infuse it with flavors and syrups.

- Ingredients:
  - 5 gal water
  - 8 lbs. white sugar
  - 1 packet yeast, such as baker's

- Directions:
  - Heat 2 gallons of water to 120 degrees Fahrenheit.

---

4   Ibid.

- Add the sugar gradually, stirring well to dissolve each addition before adding more.
- Once all sugar has been added and dissolved, dump into the fermenter and add the rest of your water (3 gallons).
- When the mixture has cooled down to 70 degrees, add baker's yeast.
- Aerate your mixture between two containers; pour into one, then another, and repeat a few times.
- Ferment at 70 degrees Fahrenheit for two weeks, maintaining a consistent temperature. You can wrap fermenter in a blanket or fermenter jacket, use space heaters in the room, etc.

- To distill:
  - Siphon into your still and begin the distillation process.

Flavored Moonshines

The simplest method for flavoring your moonshine is to add fruit directly to the jar of your finished distillation and let it sit. Cut it into slices or use fruits whole, per preference, and seal them in the jar with the moonshine, then let it sit in a cool, dark place as long as you'd like. Several months is ideal, but as little as one week can add sufficient flavor. The goal is to let your moonshine seep into the fruit and mix with the syrups and sugars. Most fruits will also color your moonshine during this process. When it comes time to serve the moonshine, you can either eat the fruit or strain it out.

Another popular method of flavoring moonshine is to add syrups or fruit juices, and even spices and other botanicals.

○ **Apple Pie Moonshine Recipe**

- Ingredients:
  - 2.5 gal apple juice
  - 2.5 gal apple cider
  - 4.5 cups white sugar
  - 4.5 cups brown sugar
  - 1 Tbsp apple pie spice, OR make your own blend:
    - ★ 1.5 tsp cinnamon
    - ★ ¾ tsp nutmeg
    - ★ ½ tsp allspice
    - ★ ¼ tsp ground gloves
  - 750mL of moonshine

- Directions:
  - Combine all ingredients EXCEPT the moonshine into a pot on your stovetop. Bring to

almost boiling.

- Cover; reduce heat to a simmer. Allow to simmer for 1 hour, stirring now and then.
- Remove pot from heat and allow mixture to cool completely.
- Once cooled, stir in your moonshine.
- Pour mixture into jars, seal, and store in the refrigerator until ready to consume.

CHAPTER 6. VIVA LA VODKA

Vodka is one of the most popular drinks out there, and with good reason: it's got a clean and smooth taste that lends it a versatility few spirits have. Think about it—what other spirit can mix so easily in both the classiest of Cosmos and the energy-drink crazies on college campuses? Not just that, but it's also easy to enjoy straight.

A Brief History

Vodka's earliest known record dates back to 1405. It was originally used for medicinal purposes, like most spirits, and had a much lower proof that was close to modern-day wine percentages. Other than this, scholars cannot agree on much in regards to vodka's origin[1].

Traditionally, vodka is made from potato or cereal grain washes. Sometimes, fruit or sugar is

---

1   Smith, A. F. The Oxford Companion to American Food and Drink. Published by Oxford University Press, 2007. p. 693.

used. When the flavor is added, it's rarely done via infusion, but rather with syrups and additives after distillation is complete.

Basic Vodka Wash Recipes

○ **Potato Vodka**[2]

- Ingredients:
  - 4 lbs. malted barley, crushed
  - 25 lbs. potatoes washed thoroughly and cut into 1" cubes
  - 5.5. gallons of water
  - 2 packets bread yeast

- Directions:
  - Put potato cubes in a large pot; cover with water and place on stovetop. Bring to boil and boil for 15 minutes.
  - Kill the heat and mash potatoes well.
  - Move the mashed potatoes and whatever liquid is left in the pot you plan to use for your mash (stainless steel pot is best).
  - Add water to reach 5.5. gallons total volume. Make sure the temperature (after adding

---

2   "How to Make Potato Vodka." Published by Clawhammer Supply Online, January 7, 2016. Accessed June 17, 2017. https://www.clawhammersupply.com/blogs/moonshine-still-blog/14516209-how-to-make-potato-vodka

water) is 140 degrees Fahrenheit; you can heat the water and add it in increments if needed, or warm mixture on the stovetop, medium heat.

- Stir in barley.
- Keep mash at 120 degrees Fahrenheit for 20 minutes.
- Stirring constantly, raise the temperature to 150 degrees.
- Leave mash at 150 for one hour. Stir now and then.
- Determine a gravity reading using a hydrometer. If it's below 1.065, add sugar until you reach this level.
- Allow mixture to cool to 75 degrees Fahrenheit.
- About 20 minutes prior to fermentation, create a yeast starter.
- Move only the liquid portion of the mash (use a marsh bag or strainer) to your sterilized fermenter.
- Add yeast starter to the fermenter.
- Add an airlock and ferment the mixture between 65-75 degrees for 2 weeks, then siphon into your still.

○ **Sugar Vodka**[3]

- Ingredients:
  - 35 to 40 cups water, hot
  - 15 lbs. white sugar
  - 7 oz yeast nutrients
  - 1 pack yeast

- Directions:
  - Add hot water to sterilize fermenter.
  - Gradually add sugar while using a sterilized stainless steel spoon to stir until dissolved.
  - Fill the fermenter with cool water to bring the temperature to 80 degrees Fahrenheit.
  - Add yeast nutrients and stir, then let mixture stand for one hour.
  - Add yeast and stir, then let mixture stand for 24 hours.
  - After 24 hours, stir mixture well (or pour between two containers).
  - Ferment mixture for 4 to 8 days before siphoning into still.

3   "Yakov's Vodka Recipe – Easy Sugar Wash." Published by Learn to Moonshine Online, January 7, 2013. Accessed June 17, 2017. http://learntomoonshine.com/yakovs-vodka-recipe-easy-sugar-wash

Making Your Own Flavored Vodkas

Vodka flavoring is done after distillation. Generally, you can simply add your infusion ingredient to a jar of vodka, let it sit 3 to 5 days (shake twice a day), and strain out infusion. Discard ingredient, unless it has dissolved. For very fine sediment, you can use a strainer lined with cheesecloth, or a coffee filter.

Some trendier infusions of late include hard candies like peppermint, hard fruit candies, chewy fruit candies, gummies, etc., which will completely dissolve in vodka, and change the color, as well.

Resist the urge to use flavor extracts like vanilla; the taste will not be as strong or pleasant as you might expect. Instead, infuse directly: vanilla bean pods will provide a much better and more complex flavoring.

That said, there are some useful shortcuts you can make that do not involve infusion. Candy flavorings (in particular, LorAnn brand; these are crafted very strongly and come in many, many varieties) can provide potent and delicious tastes. They're best used in conjunction with real infusions (putting peach candy oil in your vodka with real peaches, for example), but do very well on their own, too. The flavors available include fruits, bubble gum, cake batter, and novelties like popcorn or peanut butter.

With any new flavor combination or recipe, test small batches first to see how you like them. And in the case of candy oils, especially LorAnn brands (which are 4x stronger than traditional flavorings), remember that a little goes a long way.

CHAPTER 7. YO, HO, HO AND A BOTTLE OF RUM

Rum is distilled from molasses, a product of sugarcane. Sometimes, it can be distilled from the sugarcane itself. The highest quality rums are made from superior sugarcane and molasses, which is dictated by the soil in which it's grown. Most of the world's premium rums come from sugarcane grown in Brazil, where rum got its start.

Humble Beginnings

Rum has been around since the 17th century, when Caribbean plantation slaves fermented molasses into alcohol. Distillation came shortly after and produced rum as we know it today.

It gained popularity in the first British colonies of North America; Staten Island created the would-be country's first distillery in 1664, and

Boston soon followed suit[1].

Unlike other spirits, the type of yeast used in the fermentation of rum's sugarcane wash is extremely important; it helps dictate the rum's flavors and aromas. Light rums use fast-acting yeasts, while fuller rums are fermented with slow-acting yeasts.

After distillation, all rum is clear. While some is bottled and sold as-is in this state, most rums get aged in wooden casks for a minimum of one year; this gives the rum its complex taste and brown coloring. Sometimes, clear rum is aged in stainless steel, so it can experience similar chemical changes without the taste and color being altered by wood.

Filtering can lighten the color of aged rum, and caramel can darken it. Manufacturers tend to "match" the shade of the final product to its description - so while a very old rum might naturally come out light brown after aging, a distillery could very well choose to add caramel until the rum is dark, which gives the impression of age.

---

1   Frost, Doug. "Rum makers distill unsavory history into fresh products." Published by SFGate Online, January 6, 2005. Accessed June 18, 2017. http://www.sfgate.com/wine/spirits/article/Rum-makers-distill-unsavory-history-into-fresh-2707149.php

○ **Basic Rum Wash Recipe[2]**

- Ingredients:
    - 5½ lbs. raw sugar
    - 12½ cup molasses
    - 2.5 gallons hot water
    - 1 tsp DAP (Diammonium phosphate)
    - 1 tsp citric acid
    - 1 pack baker's yeast

- Directions:

    - Fill a large pot with hot water. Add sugar, molasses, DAP and citric acid, then stir well until the sugar and molasses completely dissolve in water.
    - Heat mixture on the stovetop to a rolling boil; remove from heat and allow to cool until it reaches 77-86 degrees Fahrenheit.
    - Transfer to fermenter; fill the remainder of the container with water of equal temperature (between 77-86 degrees Fahrenheit).
    - Measure entire wash's temp to ensure it's still within range, then add yeast and stir (if it isn't within range, warm fermenter or put wash back on the stovetop, then back into fermenter).

---

2   "Easy Rum Recipe." Published by Learn to Moonshine Online, December 30, 2012. Accessed June 18, 2017. http://learntomoonshine.com/easy-rum-recipe

- Let stand 1 hour; stir.
- Let stand for 24 hours, keeping the temp between 68 and 77 degrees Fahrenheit; stir again to aerate.
- Taste wash with a sterilized stainless spoon. When you can no longer taste sugar, fermentation is complete. Allow to sit another day or two before distillation.

- To Distill:

  - Transfer wash between bucket/pot and fermenter to aerate and remove remnants that could not be fermented. You can also use a clearing agent.
  - Distill as usual.

Aging Your Distilled Rum

To age your distilled rum, first, choose the proper container. New, fresh oak barrels that have never aged rum before giving it intense flavor and will require a much shorter aging period; older barrels that have already aged several batches take longer for the oak flavor to "seep" into that batch, yet can also provide a deeply complex flavor, since every batch that's ever been aged in it has left some behind and will pass these notes along.

Stainless steel containers will not give your rum any new flavors, but simply allow the rum to breathe and age naturally; this is good for light and clear rums.

Flavoring Your Rum

While aging is often enough to "flavor" the rum (also known as "oaking" it), some distillers do choose to add spices like nutmeg or cinnamon to their rum. You can also add fruit syrups and candy oils, or dried fruits.

Additionally, the amount of molasses or sugar in your wash recipe will dictate how strong the "rum" flavor is after distillation. Using more will give it a stronger, deeper taste.

Note: Some distillers prefer pot stills over reflux stills for rum, but you can also use your reflux still by removing some or all of the packing. Unlike other distillations, rum's flavor is enhanced with a lower reflux rate.

CHAPTER 8. OF ALL THE GIN JOINTS IN ALL THE TOWNS

Originally used as medicine in the 13th century, gin is derived from juniper berries, which give it a distinct flavor: even though different manufacturers produce many different recipes with their own unique profiles, juniper is a primary ingredient across the board.

Gin gained massive popularity as a spirit (rather than medicine, its original use) when the British government placed a heavy tax on French brandies, and simultaneously made it legal for unlicensed distillers to produce and sell gin. This time is referred to as the Gin Craze, and lasted from 1695 to 1735. In 1736, the government started requiring a license to distill gin once more. They also imposed a heavy tax on the spirit; this led to illegal distillations from private residences, which were flavored with turpentine.

Making Gin

Column-distilled gin is made with washes from grain, sugar beets, potatoes, sugarcane, grapes, or white sugar, and is then redistilled with juniper and other flavorings (such as lemon peel, anise, cinnamon, etc.) in a pot still using a "gin basket." You can also use an essence still, such as a modified coffee pot. The result is a lightly flavored gin known as distilled gin or London dry gin[1].

○ **Basic Gin Recipe[2]**

- Use a vodka wash recipe (like the potato or sugar one in this book in chapter 4) and distill as usual.

- Ingredients:
    - 2 cups vodka
    - 2 Tbsp juniper berries
    - ½ tsp coriander seeds
    - 1 tsp chamomile

1   "The Gin Craze," audio broadcast by the BBC. Aired December 15, 2016. Accessed online June 19, 2017 via http://www.bbc.co.uk/programmes/b084zk6z
2   Simmons, Marcia. "Basic Gin Recipe." Published by Serious Eats Online. Accessed June 19, 2017. http://www.seriouseats.com/recipes/2012/06/how-to-make-your-own-gin-recipe-juniper-infusion-easy-homemade-gin.html

- ½ tsp lavender
- 3 cardamom pods, broken
- 1 whole bay leaf
- 4 allspice berries
- Two 4-inch pieces grapefruit peel with no pith

- Directions:
  - Combine vodka and juniper berries in a glass jar. Seal; allow to steep for 12 hours.
  - Add all additional ingredients; reseal jar, shake, and steep for 36 more hours.
  - Strain out solids through a cheesecloth- or coffee-filter-lined strainer, then strain again into a container of choice.
  - Store at room temperature up to one year.

- *Note:* you can also use a pot still and gin botanicals basket to re-distill the vodka, with all ingredients in the basket, so flavors infuse into new distillation and you don't have to strain them out.

Other Flavors

Gin is a spirit that heavily relies on infusion for its unique flavor, so experiment with your own unique combinations! You can increase, decrease, and substitute infusions at will, as long as juniper is included (since this is what makes gin...well, gin). Some additions to try to include cubeb berries, Grains of Paradise, cassia bark, cinnamon, lime peel, and black pepper. Some will require a bit of a hunt, but many are ingredients sitting in your spice rack right now.

If you don't have a botanicals basket or pot still, you can make a basket with copper mesh to sit in the middle of the column in your reflux still.

CHAPTER 9. WHERE'S THE WHISKEY?

Whiskey is one of the most popular spirits in the world[1], and has enjoyed that title for thousands of years! It's smooth but strong and is nearly as versatile as vodka—perhaps even more so, just in different ways.

In America, the whiskey and bourbon industry has sales over $3 billion annually. This number is proportionately similar in many other countries, as well, and each region seems to have its own unique and much-loved whiskey lining the shelves.

---

1   "Scotch Whiskey Imports Hit Record Level." Published by Scotch Whisky Association Online, April 2, 2013. Accessed June 20, 2017. https://web.archive.org/web/20130523183816/http://www.scotch-whisky.org.uk/documents/scotch-whisky-exports-hit-record-level/

The Origin of Whiskey

Whiskey might have gotten its start as early as the 2nd millennium, BC, in Mesopotamia, although whiskey, as we know it today, has no clear origin. The first mention of whiskey in Scotland is from 1494; in Ireland, 1405. Back then, whiskey was not aged. It tasted harsh, and its high potency was linked to many deaths—but still, its popularity climbed upward.

In 1725, the British imposed such high taxes on whiskey that citizens began distilling it in secrecy. During the American Prohibition from 1920 to 1933, whiskey was only legally available as a prescription from one's doctor. The product being sold was close to what we call moonshine, rather than whiskey; while it was corn-based and high-proof, it wasn't aged due to high demand.

Aging: What Turns Young Moonshine into Old Whiskey

The process of aging whiskey began later. With smoother flavor profiles and richer colors, aged whiskeys became very popular, very fast. Soon, aging was the standard for quality whiskey.

Aging consists of putting whiskey in oak casks for a year or more to allow it to undergo a six-part process: extraction, evaporation, oxidation, concentration, filtration, and coloration. It changes not only the taste and color of the whiskey, but also its chemical makeup.

Usually, casks are made of charred white oak. This provides a beautiful amber coloring (which can vary in intensity) and enhances the distillation's unique flavors, which are largely dictated by the type of mash it was created from. Most whiskeys are made from malted grains (malted whiskey) but don't have to be.

Regional Whiskeys

Whiskey's popularity is due, in part, to its regional variations. There are different types of whiskey for many countries and areas, some of which have distinct factors to set it apart from the rest.

- Irish Whiskey - typically distilled three times, then aged a minimum of three years by Irish law.
- Scotch whiskey - typically distilled twice; also required to age three years or more. Manufacturers are mandated, by law, to label the age according to the youngest whiskey within

that blend.

- American whiskey - cannot be distilled to anything higher than 80% ABV, and must be barreled at 125 proof or less. Coloring or flavoring is not allowed in the final product (only water, to dilute alcohol content if needed). Must be aged in new charred-oak barrels, with the exception of clear corn whiskey, which is often sold as "legal moonshine" instead. Unlike Ireland or Scotland, the US government does not dictate how long American whiskey must be aged.
- Tennessee whiskey: a popular subcategory of American whiskey, this includes Jack Daniel's, Collier and McKeel, and others. Whiskey is filtered through charcoal and technically classified as bourbon under the North American Fair Trade Agreement.
- Canadian whiskey is also incredibly popular in America, thanks to its accessibility via "rum runners" (illegal importers) during Prohibition[2].

There are many other regional variations of whiskey, and each country has unique regulations distilleries must adhere to in order to sell their product legally.

---

2   "Whisky." Published by Wikipedia, multiple authors. Accessed June 20, 2017. https://en.wikipedia.org/wiki/Whisky

Types of Whiskey

- Single malt: made with one type of malted grain.
- Blended malt: a mixture of single-malt batches.
- Single cask: unmixed, bottled from one batch from one cask.

○ **Whiskey Corn Wash Recipe** [3]

- Ingredients:

    - 8.5 lbs. corn, additive-free and crushed
    - 5 gallons water
    - 2 lbs. malted barley, crushed
    - 1 package bread yeast

- Directions:

    - Heat 5 gal water to 165 degrees Fahren-

---

3   "How to Make a Corn Mash: 11 Easy Steps that Will Make a Great Corn Whiskey." Published by Learn to Moonshine Online, November 24, 2014. Accessed June 21, 2017. http://learntomoonshine. com/how-to-make-a-corn-mash-11-easy-steps-that-will-make-a-great-corn-whiskey

heit; kill the heat.

- Add crushed corn to water; stir for 2-3 minutes, then every 5 minutes until the temperature has cooled to 152 degrees Fahrenheit. Corn has started to gel, thanks to its starches releasing into the water.
- Add malted barley, stir for one minute.
- Cover with lid and let sit for 1.5 hours.
- At about the 1-hour mark, prepare a yeast starter.
- After the 1.5 hours has passed, strain mash through cheesecloth to remove solids.
- Aerate mixture between two buckets or pour into the carboy and shake vigorously for one minute.
- When the temp is between 75-85 degrees Fahrenheit, pour into the fermenter.
- Add yeast starter.
- Install airlock and allow to ferment for 1-2 weeks, until bubbling stops.
- Distill as usual.

• To Age[4]:

  - Pour into prepped oak barrel(s) and seal; allow to age at least 2 weeks.
  - Note: be careful when aging whiskey; you

4   "How to Make Your Own Aged Whiskey." Published by Clawhammer Supply Online, May 4, 2013. Accessed June 21, 2017. https://www.clawhammersupply.com/blogs/moonshine-still-blog/7813667-how-to-make-your-own-aged-whiskey

can "over-oak" your batch and disturb the flavor. Draw a small sample every few weeks to determine how oaky the flavor is, and if it needs to be aged longer or if it's ready to bottle.

- You can buy pre-made whiskey barrels or aging kits, which allow you to build your own barrel with minimal tools and carpentry skills. Generally speaking, it is not cost-effective to build your own from scratch. As a "cheat," some distillers put charred oak chips into their containers, then strain them out with coffee filters after aging.

CHAPTER 10. TEQUILA TIME

Tequila is distilled from the blue agave plant, which produces a great deal of sugar in its core. Its name comes from the city of Tequila in Guadalajara, Mexico, its place of origin, where it got its start in the

16th century after Spanish conquistadors ran out of brandy and tried distilling their own.

The first tequila factory was opened in 1600, in modern-day Jalisco. It was exported to the US in the late 1800s. Originally known as "tequila extract," it became known as simply "tequila" in the American market, its common name all over today.

The Painstaking Production of Tequila

Tequila's production begins with the planting and cultivation of the blue agave plant. Jimadores, the men who raise and harvest the plant, are taught generationally; raising agave is often a family business, passed down over centuries.

The core, or pina, is carefully cut away after harvest when it has just the right amount of sugars. The pinas are baked in ovens to break down these sugars, then shredded or mashed with a stone wheel; the juice is extracted, poured into vats, and allowed to ferment into a wort until it's ready to distill.

This first distillation produces an "ordinario" tequila; a second distillation makes a "silver" tequila, which is clear. Law mandates at least two distillations. Three distillations are sometimes done, but rarely, as this removes a great deal of the agave flavor. Silver tequila can be sold as-is or allowed to age in wooden barrels[1].

Types of Tequila

- Blanco: white or "silver" tequila, unaged. Bottled immediately after its second distillation.
- Joven: "young" or "gold" tequila, unaged but flavored; sometimes a result of aged tequila being blended with silver.
- Reposado: "rested." This is aged at least two months, but less than a year.
- Anejo: vintage/aged. Aged more than a year, but less than three years; only aged in small barrels.
- Extra Anejo: Aged at least three years in oak barrels. The older a tequila is, the smoother its flavor; it's also more complex.

---

1   Chadwick, Ian. "Culivation and Agriculture." In Search of the Blue Agave. Accessed online June 21, 2017, via http://www.ianchadwick.com/tequila/cultivation.htm

- ○ **Basic "Tequila" Recipe**[2]

- Note: it is illegal, even with all pertinent permits for other liquors, to make true tequila outside of the five Mexican states where blue agave grows. This recipe is NOT for "true" tequila, but is more of an "agave moonshine" using blue agave nectar. This is because blue agave shoots are incredibly expensive and hard to find; most sellers will not even distribute them outside of Mexico.

- Ingredients:

  - 92 oz blue agave nectar
  - 2 lbs cane sugar
  - 2 gal water
  - 1 packet bread yeast
  - 1 tsp FerMax yeast nutrient (optional, but recommended)
  - Yellow food coloring (optional)

- Directions:

  - Heat 2 gallons of water in the large stainless pot to just before boiling. Add sugar and stir

2   "How to Make a Tequila Wash/Mash." Video tutorial by Platt R. Productions, published April 9, 2016. Accessed June 21, 2017. https://www.youtube.com/watch?v=g0DQ4ds9IEU

until dissolved.
- Stir in agave nectar.
- Remove mixture from heat. Add to the fermenter and fill with water until it reaches 5 gallons total.
- Add yeast and FerMax and stir.
- Cover; let sit one hour. Stir.
- Cover and allow mixture to ferment for 5 to 7 days.
- Distill. If desired, distill twice.
- Add food coloring for the desired color; bottle.

CHAPTER 11. BRANDY, LIQUEURS, AND OTHER EXCUSES TO SPEND MORE TIME IN THE STILL HOUSE

Brandy

Brandy is made by distilling wine and sometimes aged in casks or colored with caramel. It's a popular after-dinner spirit and is often enjoyed straight at room temperature, or warmed in teas, ciders, and more. Cognac, Armagnac, and other spirits are brandies from specific areas, hence their names.

Brandy is as old as distillation itself; since it's made from fruit mashes, it would have been one of the mankind's earliest spirits. By the 15th century, brandy distillation had grown in popularity and begun to replace its diluted predecessors.

Most brandy is made from grapes; all start

as "base wines," which are not the same as table wines (wines you drink). Base wines have a smaller amount of sulfur, less sugar, and higher acidity; they're usually made from young grapes[1].

Sunchoke Spirit

Sunchokes, also known as Jerusalem artichokes, are a type of sunflower found in eastern North America. The spirit made from these is technically a type of brandy, although it's very rare and is distinct enough to deserve its own category.

○ **Brandy Recipe**[2]

Making the Wine

- Ingredients:

  - 3 quarts of fruit, such as pears, peaches, grapes, etc.
  - Sugar, if using berries
  - 6 tsp active dry yeast
  - 7 cups water, 1 cup warm and 6 cups cold

1   "Brandy." Wikipedia. Accssed June 22, 2017. https://en.wikipedia.org/wiki/Brandy
2   "How to Make Brandy." Published by Learn to Moonshine Online, January 18, 2016. Accessed June 23, 2017. http://learntomoonshine.com/how-to-make-brandy

- Directions:

  - Wash and cut fruit into small slices. Discard pits or seeds and stems; you can leave skins on.
  - Mash fruit in a glass bowl with potato masher.
  - If using berries, add sugar by putting a layer in the bottom of your bowl, then a layer of berries, then a layer of sugar, etc., until all fruit is covered. Mash.
  - Add yeast to 1 cup warm water; stir. Add to fruit, then stir in 6 cups cold water.
  - Cover and allow to sit in a cool place for four weeks, stirring every 7 days or so.
  - Bottle wine until it's time for distillation.

Distilling the Wine

- Be sure to leave 1/4 of still empty, as wine tends to bubble during the process and will rise.
- Turn heat on high to start; as soon as alcohol starts coming from the spout, reduce heat to a low simmer until 1 drop comes out ever 1-3 seconds.
- Discard foreshots/head, which is toxic (first 7.5 ml per 1.5 L of wine).
- After discarding heads, the hearts will begin to

collect and come out of the spout. The hearts are clear and will smell vaguely of fruit; you should collect about 30 mL per 1.5 L of wine. Collect only this, then switch containers.

- The remainder of the product will be the tails, which is milky and likely won't smell of fruit. Discard this portion, or stop distilling before/ shortly after it begins condensing.
- Store hearts/brandy in a jar at cool temperature until ready to enjoy, unless aging first.

Aging Your Distillation

If you choose to age your brandy, you can use a white oak barrel like you'd use for whiskey, or mix toasted wood chips like cherry into your brandy in glass containers. Cover with a coffee filter and rubber bands until brandy has achieved the desired color and flavor you'd like, which can take 2-4 weeks or more. Pull small amounts for tasting through the aging process.

Liqueurs

Liqueurs are distilled spirits sweetened and flavored with fruit, cream, or spices. They are not aged. This group includes cordials and schnapps in the US, although other countries have different meanings for those names (in Germany, for example, Schnapps is a type of brandy).

Liqueurs are usually not very strong and tend to be mixed in cocktails rather than consumed straight. Some can have quite high proofs, though, and a few are enjoyed as "sipping liqueurs," like Bailey's Irish Cream, Grand Marnier, or blends like Tuaca.

Originally used as herbal medicines, the earliest forms of liqueur as we know it, were prepared in Italian monasteries as early as the 13th century.

○ **Peach Schnapps (American) Recipe**[3]

Note: German Schnapps is essentially brandy; this recipe is for the sweet, peach liqueur known as peach schnapps in America.

• Ingredients:

- 1 cups moonshine
- 2 large peaches
- 1 Tbsp lemon juice
- ¾ cup water

---

3   "Homemade Peach Schnapps." Published by Crunchy, Creamy Sweet June 17, 2015. Accessed June 25, 2017. http://www.crunchycreamysweet.com/2015/06/17/homemade-peach-schnapps/

- ¾ cup sugar

• Directions:

- Wash and pit peaches. Cut into slices.
- Place peaches into a tall glass container, preferably one with a sealing lid (mason jars or swing-top jars will work well).
- Add moonshine and lemon juice.
- Allow to sit for 24 hours.
- In saucepan, mix sugar and water. Heat on medium heat until boiling.
- Boil for 30 seconds and remove from heat.
- Cool completely and add to peaches and alcohol mixture.
- Let sit for 24 hours. Store in fridge until ready to consume.

Other Uses For Your Distillation Skills

Stills can also be used to distill water and filter out impurities or create perfumes. To extract a scent, you can use your reflux still with water and a botanicals basket (or one made from copper wire mesh in the column) filled with the plant of choice. The distilled product is known as essence and can make a potent base for homemade perfumes.

NOTE: reflux stills are not commonly used to extract scent or distill water, but it is possible. Adjust packing material as needed.

The Farm Distillery

Farm distilleries used to be very common, but have diminished with the decline in agriculture. Today, most farm distilleries are merely extensions of regular farms, which sell their crops and use unsellable ones/excess to produce alcohol[4].

You can have a "farm to flask" operation as well by growing your own crops to use in your mashes and washes, to produce the product 100% from start to finish. While not all climates allow for certain crops to grow, potatoes are a relatively easy and versatile crop and can be grown in very small gardens or even buckets.

---

4   "What is a Farm Distillery?" Published by Distillery Trail Online, April 20, 2015. Accessed June 26, 2017. http://www. distillerytrail.com/blog/what-is-a-farm-distillery/

CHAPTER 12. MIXERS AND BITTERS

Nothing says "fully-stocked bar" like those extra little touches, from fragrant bitters to a bevy of mixers!

Mixers are non-alcoholic liquids that can be added to alcohol to change the flavor, enhance existing flavors, lower the alcohol content, or even change the drink's viscosity or temperature (ex: milk in White Russians, coffee with Bailey's, etc.). Common mixers include fruit juices and sodas, as well as caffeinated beverages like coffee or energy drinks. Simple syrups, grenadine, and lime juice are some mixers that are not consumed alone and are made in a concentrated, thicker form; their primary ingredient is sugar, so they add a sweetness and sometimes additional flavors to the cocktails.

Bitters are alcohol infused with botanical essences; they have a bitter or sour taste or are sometimes bittersweet. Originally, they were used as medicine. They are commonly consumed straight as after-dinner drinks or mixed into cocktails.

Make Your Own Bitters[1]

- Combine 2 quarts of your distilled vodka or whiskey with spices, roots, barks, etc., of your choice in a jar.
- Seal and allow to sit for two weeks. Shake daily.
- After steeping is complete, strain through a cheesecloth-lined strainer (or coffee filters) into a clean container, then seal.
- Take remnants you strained out and heat stove with some water then put into separate jar and seal.
- Allow both jars to sit 1 week. Shake the water-and-remnants jar daily.
- Strain water from remnants jar and mix water with your vodka or whiskey infusion; discard the remnants/solids you strained out.
- Strain liquid through cheesecloth until it is no longer murky. If desired, add simple syrup to taste and shake well.
- Allow to sit for three days.
- Bottle bitters in dropper bottles prior to use.

---

1   Archibald, Anna."Ever Make Your Own Bitters? You Should." Published by Liquor.com February 5, 2015. Accessed June 26, 2017. http://www.liquor.com/articles/make-your-own-bitters/#gs.WWXrQbk

Common spices and ingredients to use[2] include:

- Spices

    - Allspice
    - Anise
    - Aniseed
    - Caraway
    - Cardamom
    - Cassia
    - Celery seed
    - Chiles
    - Cloves
    - Ginger
    - Juniper berries
    - Nutmeg
    - Vanilla beans/pods

- Herbs and Flowers

    - Chamomile
    - Hibiscus
    - Hops
    - Lavender
    - Lemongrass

---

2   Han, Emily. "How to Make Homemade Bitters." Published by the Kitchn Online, December 5, 2013. Accessed June 27, 2017. http://www.thekitchn.com/how-to-make-homemade-bitters-cooking-lessons-from-the-kitchn-197883

- Mint
- Rose
- Rosemary
- Sage
- Thyme

• Dried fruits or peels
• Nuts
• Beans
  - Cacao
  - Cocoa nibs
  - Coffee

Cocktails to Try

Once you've gotten the hang of distillation, why not host a fancy party to share your creations? Check out our cocktail book (available at the end of this book) for cocktail recipes you can make with your distillations, homemade cordials, bitters, mixers, and more!

CHAPTER 13. ADVANCED DISTILLATION

As your skills become more advanced, so can your still! Fractioning stills-essentially very tall reflux stills-separate, or fraction, the heads, middle and tail runs of your distillations, so you don't have to quickly switch containers to collect each in order. It's good for beginners to start on regular reflux stills, though, so they can learn what heads or foreshots, which are toxic, look and smell like; it's also good to know what impure tails look like, if applicable to what you're distilling.

When you've tried enough recipes, you'll start to notice a pattern among them - what works, what doesn't, how much to use of what, etc., and might be eager to make some mashes of your own invention. As long as you're following the safety and sanitization rules of all distilling, try anything you can think of!

Many distillers move into more complicated spirits, like absinthe, or try to replicate top-shelf versions of their old favorites, using higher quality ingredients and more involved processes.

CHAPTER 14. SOME NOTES ON BOTTLING, PRESERVATION, AND STORAGE

- For most spirits, storing in a glass container with a sealed lid (mason jars, swing top jars or bottles, corked bottles, etc.) is plenty. Keep in cool, dark areas (or room temp, at most) to avoid evaporation.
- Some alcohol can be stored indefinitely; others, up to a year, depending on what it's made with.
- Note: do not use sealing containers (with rubber/ foam seals around the edge or on lid) to catch and discard heads/foreshots. Because the alcohol content is toxically high in these, they can deteriorate the seals.
- For long-term storage, or to give alcohol as gifts, many distillers prefer glass bottles with corks. Because corks are porous, evaporation over time is a potential concern; many people dip the bottles in wax to seal them for long-term storage, or to make good-looking gifts their recipients won't have to drink right away.
- While it's very rare for alcohol to spoil, it can happen. You'll notice discoloration and the strange separation of the components, particularly in fruit liqueurs with lower proofs. If your alcohol spoils, throw it out. The same goes for washes and marshes, which can spoil during or after fermentation (especially if your equipment was not sterilized before using).
- When using corks, be aware that they can dry out and shrink over time. Try to keep the liquid inside the bottle in contact with the cork, by lay-

ing the bottle on its side during storage. After opening, consume within a few days.

- Unless you're aging alcohol in a barrel for a long time, consume your products within 3 years. Storing them longer than that will allow the small bit of oxygen in the container (trapped during transfer, which is unavoidable) to oxidize and spoil the contents. Some distillers success-fully store their alcohol 5 years or longer, but unless you're using preservatives like you'd find in commercial liquors, this is rare.

Federal, state and local laws wrap miles of red tape around private distillers. You need a special license and must be qualified as a craft distillery - in other words, an actual business, and one which pays some hefty taxes on their products.

Every new formula must be approved by your state government, which can take several months. From invention to selling, the process of a new product approval will last 6 months, at the least.

The Case for Making Non-commercial Distilling Legal

Overall, distillation for personal (non-commercial) use has the most ridiculous amount of red tape, since distillers don't intend to sell it. There are so many rules and regulations, it discourages people from even trying-and those rules only exist because the government wants people to buy liquor, not make it. Commercial liquors are taxed and generate local and national revenue; home distillation doesn't. What's more, beer and wine-which are far easier to make legally in your home-have smaller taxes on them when compared to spirits[1]. This is why beer and wine production is not regulated nearly as heavily.

---

1   Tsai, Michelle. "Why is Moonshine Against the Law?" Published by Slate Online October 18, 2007. Accessed June 27, 2017. http://www.slate.com/articles/news_and_politics/explainer/2007/10/why_is_moonshine_against_the_law.html

What You CAN Do (Legally)

Unless you have a license and are classified as a distillery, you cannot legally sell homemade alcohol of any kind. You can, however, give it away, or use it to barter for services and products.

However, just because you can't sell it, doesn't mean you can't have a brand! You can design customized jar and bottle labels on sites like vistaprint.com, purchase wax seal stamps with unique logos or initials, and even hand out business cards and start a website about your products. These can make your hobby, feel even more fulfilling, and make the final product look very professional. And if you decide to become a licensed distiller and distributor, later on, a lot of your promo work will be much easier.

You can also enter spirit competitions, where your product will be tested and evaluated. These contests often have cash prizes. Some are only available to licensed distilleries, so make sure to check the rules on whether or not private distillers can enter.

CONCLUSION. CHEERS! THE FUTURE OF TRUE CRAFT DISTILLING

Craft distillation is on the rise, especially with the increase in popularity of home-brewed beers and wines. These are paving the way for home distillation and small businesses, and it's probable that some of that troublesome red tape will be taken down in the next few years.

In 2015, there were over 1,200 craft distilleries, three times the amount of 2007. An estimated 300 distilleries open each year in America[1].

Some distilleries negotiate buyouts with big-name corporations, which includes the sale of their formulas. Others operate just fine on their own and work on growing their business from within. Thanks to the internet, craft distilleries can ship their product all over, and get the word out more easily than via the grapevine.

Thanks to changing state laws, some distill-

_____

1   Eaton, Dan. "Craft Spirits vs. Craft Beer." Published by Columbus Business First Online, September 23, 2009. Accessed June 28, 2017. http://www.bizjournals.com/columbus/news/2016/09/23/craft-spirits-vs-craft-beer-there-are-parallels.html

eries can now open on-site bars and restaurants, where customers can sample and purchase their products straight from the source.

While it's not likely that craft distilleries will ever pull in the big money of corporate names, it is possible they could turn into as viable businesses as craft breweries have become in recent years. The main difference between the two is the barrier to entry: simply put, making beer is easier, and doesn't require the same patience as distillation or aging. But for the few distillers who stick with it, navigate the correct channels, and have just the right stroke of luck, success is waiting.

DIY BARTENDER:

COCKTAILS FOR THE
HOMEMADE MIXOLOGIST

CHAPTER 1. MOONSHINE

Moonshine is a rather strong distillation made from a corn-based wash. In fact, before it's aged in barrels, whiskey is technically moonshine!

Because it isn't infused with wood flavors or aged to change its chemical makeup, moonshine has a less complex taste than whiskey-but that makes it ideal for cocktails and infusions! Put some 'shine in a shaker and enjoy one (or all) of these moonshine mixtures.

Full Blue Moon

- 1 oz moonshine
- 1 oz blue curaçao
- 2 oz lemon-lime soda

Combine in shaker with ice; shake to blend. Pour into rocks glass or tumbler and garnish with maraschino spear or lemon peel, if desired.

Peachy Keen Lemonade

- Peach-infused moonshine*
- Lemonade
- Lemon wedges, if desired

Mix 1 part moonshine with 2 parts lemonade in a pitcher. Chill for 20 minutes before serving over ice; garnish with lemon wedges.

*To infuse moonshine: fill mason jar with moonshine and 2-4 cups of peach pieces. Allow to steep for 3 days or more, shaking twice a day. Strain out peaches before drinking, or eat pieces as additional treat! You can also infuse your moonshine with other fruits or herbs like lavender, mint, and more.

Shamrock Shock

- 1 oz moonshine
- ½ oz Midori melon liqueur

Pour both ingredients in a sugar-rimmed shot glass. If desired, use kiwi-infused moonshine.

Moonshine Mimosa

- 1 ½ oz moonshine
- 4 oz orange juice
- 2 ½ seltzer water or lemon-lime soda
- strawberries or other fresh fruit (optional)

Pour all ingredients in champagne flute over fresh fruit slices; stir with straw.

Lemon Drop Shine Shooter

- 1 ½ oz moonshine
- ½ to 1 oz lemon juice
- ½ oz simple syrup (optional)
- rimming sugar

Pour moonshine, lemon juice, and simple syrup (if desired) into shaker with ice. Shake well to combine. Wet rim of shooter or rocks glass; dip in rimming sugar to coat. Strain shaker into glass.

CHAPTER 2. VODKA

Potato- or sugar-based, straight or mixed, flavored or plain: vodka's one of the world's most popular spirits, and with good reason! Its versatility is owed to its pure flavor and ability to mix into just about any drink. Diehard vodka fans even enjoy this over ice or in a glass as-is, no additions needed.

Of course, even the smoothest vodka can get dull. If you want to shake things up, try one of our vodka cocktails, from classic favorites to trendy new mixes.

Classic Cosmo

- 1 ½ oz vodka
- ½ oz triple sec
- ½ oz lime juice
- 1 oz cranberry juice

Put all ingredients into ice-filled shaker and shake to blend. Strain into martini glass; garnish with lime peel, if desired.

Moscow Mule

The traditional recipe for a Moscow Mule contains the following ingredients:

- 1/4 oz. lime juice (one lime wedge squeezed)
- 2 ounces vodka
- 4 to 6 ounces ginger beer

Pour vodka and lime juice into copper mug. Add ginger beer and ice, if desired; stir with stirring stick. Garnish with lime wedge, if desired. Moscow Mule drink is served over ice.

When you handle the copper mug, it maintains drink temperature with your Moscow Mule safely chilled inside.

Using copper mugs for Moscow Mule cocktail enhances the vodka flavors and the individual flavor of the ginger beer and lime. When vodka and copper walls make contact, the copper begins to oxidize and slightly boosts the aroma and enhances the taste.

We recommend to buy the Moscow mule mugs set. Modeled after original Moscow Mule mugs from 1940s these mugs work great for chilled beer, iced coffee, lemonade, and iced tea, as well as any vodka, gin, rum, tequila, or whiskey cocktails you can imagine. Also great as a normal drinking glass for water.

Sex on the Beach

- 1 ½ oz vodka
- ½ oz peach schnapps
- ½ oz pineapple juice
- 1 ½ oz cranberry juice

Put ingredients in ice-filled shaker and shake well. Strain into highball glass over new ice. Garnish with orange wheel or maraschino cherry, if desired.

Sweet Vodka Spritzer

- 1 oz vodka
- 4 oz moscato
- 1-3 oz strawberry soda

Mix ingredients into ice-filled glass. Stir with spoon or straw; add fresh strawberries, if desired.

Dirty Shirley

- 2 oz vodka
- 4 oz lemon-lime soda
- 1 tsp grenadine
- 2-4 maraschino cherries to taste

Put all ingredients except cherries into ice-filled shaker and shake well. Strain into tumbler over new ice and cherries. Top with additional cherries or lime wedges, if desired.

CHAPTER 3. WHISKEY AND BOURBON

Some whiskey aficionados consider it sacrilege to pair whiskey with anything other than a water back or a little ice-and sometimes, not even then-but we love the taste of carefully crafted whiskey cocktails! The right blend of flavors can enhance a good whiskey's complexity, draw out certain notes, and make a whiskey lover out of anyone.

Whiskey Sour

- 1 ½ oz whiskey
- ¾ oz lemon juice
- ¾ oz simple syrup
- maraschino cherry and lemon wedge (optional)

Combine all ingredients in ice-filled shaker and shake well. Strain into rocks glass over new ice. Garnish with cherry and lemon wedge, if desired.

Old Fashioned

- 2 oz rye whiskey or bourbon
- 2-3 dashes bitters
- sugar cube
- splash of club soda

Place sugar cube in rocks glass. Wet with bitters and club soda, then crush sugar with spoon. Turn glass so sugars and bitters coat it. Add large ice cube and pour in rye or bourbon. Serve with stirring straw and garnish with orange wedge and maraschino cherry, if desired.

Mint Julep

- 2 ½ oz whiskey
- 2 splashes of seltzer water
- 10 or so fresh, whole mint leaves
- 1-2 tsp sugar

Put all but one mint leaf in rocks glass, followed by sugar. Muddle well until leaves are no longer whole. Add 1 splash seltzer water, then fill glass almost full with ice. Add bourbon; top with remaining seltzer. Stir and garnish with remaining mint leaf, if desired.

Tennessee Lemonade

- 8 oz whiskey
- 4 cups water
- 4 oz honey
- 5 lemons

Heat water in small pot on stovetop. Just before boiling, add honey and stir until it's dissolved. Remove from heat. Squeeze juice from lemons into honey water and stir well. Allow to cool completely. Pour into pitcher; add whiskey and stir. Store in fridge until ready to serve by pouring over ice in tumbler glasses. Garnish with lemon twists, if desired. Make about 4 8-oz servings.

CHAPTER 3. WHISKEY AND BOURBON

Other than margaritas or the occasional Tequila Sunrise, most people wouldn't dream of mixing up a cocktail with tequila-but maybe that's because they've never seen recipes like these! Our recipes will work best with true tequila, but can also be made from the agave moonshine recipe we included in Raising the Bar: The Home Distiller's Workbook

Mintequila Brew

- 2 oz tequila
- 4-6 oz cold coffee
- 2 oz crème de menthe
- 1-2 vanilla bean pods (optional)

Pour tequila and coffee into ice-filled shaker and shake well. Strain into tumbler glass over new ice, then add crème de menthe and stir lightly with straw.

Optional: infuse your tequila for 24 hours beforehand with vanilla pods, split length-wise.

Ginger Shooter

- 2 oz tequila
- 2 oz ginger beer
- 1-2 dashes ginger or citrus bitters

Pour all ingredients into ice-filled shaker and shake well. Strain into empty rocks glass.

Blackberry Slammer

- 8 oz water
- ½ to ¾ cup white sugar
- 1 cup blackberries, rinsed
- 2 oz tequila
- 2 oz club soda or lemon-lime soda

Pour water, sugar, and blackberries into pot on stovetop and heat over medium heat until boiling. Reduce heat; simmer for 8 to 11 minutes, stirring occasionally, until sugar is dissolved and black-berries have started to break down. Add addition-al sugar if mixture is too runny; it should have the consistency of syrup as it simmers.

Remove from heat. Mash blackberries with wooden spoon, strain out with a fine mesh strain-er.

Discard blackberries. Allow syrup to cool com-pletely, then pour into glass jar with lid or swing-top jar.

Put tequila, soda, and 1 tsp to 1 Tbsp of black-berry syrup in an ice-filled shaker. Shake well to combine, then strain over new ice into rocks glass. Garnish with fresh blackberries, if desired.

Store remaining blackberry syrup in fridge for up to one month. Bonus: you can also use it as a pancake or ice cream topping!

Tequila Summer Slush

- 4 oz tequila
- 2 cups ice
- ½ seedless cucumber, finely chopped
- 2 oz lime juice
- 4 mint leaves
- up to 4 oz lemon-lime soda

Put all ingredients except soda into blender. Pulse to chop up ice, then blend until all ingredients are combined. Add lemon-lime soda if desired to reach preferred consistency. Pour into tall glasses and serve with straws and cucumber wheels as garnish. Makes about 2 8-oz servings or 4 4 oz-servings.

CHAPTER 5. BRANDY

Brandy, made from distilled wine, is delicious on its own - but it can also be the perfect addition to cocktails, hot or cold! Here are some ways to enjoy this spirit, any time of the year.

Hard Iced Cider

- 2 oz brandy
- 2 oz apple cider
- 1-2 dashes bitters
- ½ oz dry vermouth
- cinnamon sticks (optional)

Combine all ingredients in ice-filled shaker and shake well. Pour over new ice in rocks glass; garnish with cinnamon stick, if desired.

Hot Toddy for One

- 2 oz brandy
- 1-2 tsp sugar to taste
- 6 oz water
- pinch of cinnamon or nutmeg

Heat water in kettle or on stovetop until boiling; remove from heat. Stir in sugar until dissolved. Pour into mug and add brandy. Top with a pinch of spices, if desired.

Vanilla Roobios Hard Tea

- 6 oz rooibos tea, brewed and hot
- 1-2 vanilla pods, split length-wise
- 2 oz brandy

Put vanilla pods into brewed tea and let steep for 10-20 minutes. Remove pods and reheat tea on stovetop. Remove from heat and pour into mugs; top with brandy.

Iced version: do not reheat vanilla-infused tea, but instead allow to cool completely. Put in ice-filled shaker with brandy and shake well, then pour into glass over new ice.

Dirty Mother

- 2 oz brandy
- 1 oz Kahlua
- 1 oz cream or whole milk
- pinch of nutmeg or cinnamon for garnish (optional)

Combine all ingredients in ice-filled shaker and shake well. Strain into martini glass and top with dash of spice, if desired.

ABOUT THE AUTHOR

Jim O'Brien is a home distiller and author from Minnesota. When he isn't writing or perfecting his latest batch of moonshine, Jim and his wife, their two children, and two Greyhounds enjoy camping, fishing, and cycling. His works include Raise the Bar: The Home Distiller's Guide, and DIY Bartender: Cocktails for the Homemade Mixologist.

THANK YOU FOR PURCHASING THIS BOOK!

I also have one small favor to ask you. I'd really appreciate it if you could take just a few seconds to leave a review on this book. It really affects my ability to be successful and would be greatly appreciated.

Your unbiased, honest feedback helps ensure me keep doing things right and encourages to keep sharing helpful tips!

Thank you, good luck!

Sincerely yours,
Jim O'Brien

Made in the USA
Middletown, DE
07 January 2021

30960430R00068